MUSTARD

MUSTARD

southwater

This edition published by Southwater

Distributed in the UK by
The Manning Partnership
Batheaston, Bath BA1 7RL, UK
tel. (0044) 01225 852 727
fax. (0044) 01225 852 852

Distributed in the USA by
Ottenheimer Publishing
5 Park Center Court
Suite 300
Owing Mills MD 2117-5001, USA
tel. (001) 410 902 9100
fax. (001) 410 902 7210

Distributed in Australia by
Sandstone Publishing
56 John Street, Leichhardt
New South Wales 2040, Australia
tel. (0061) 2 9552 3815
fax. (0061) 2 9552 1538

Distributed in New Zealand by
Five Mile Press NZ
Unit 3/46a Taharoto Road, PO Box 33-1071
Takapuna, Auckland 9, New Zealand
tel. (0064) 9 486 1925
fax. (0064) 9 486 1454

Southwater is an imprint of
Anness Publishing Limited
© 1998, 2000 Anness Publishing Limited
1 3 5 7 9 10 8 6 4 2

Publisher: Joanna Lorenz
Senior Cookery Editor: Linda Fraser
Project Editor: Margaret Malone
Designer: Bill Mason
Illustrations: Anna Koska

Photographers: William Adams-Lingwood, Steve Baxter, James Duncan, Michelle Garrett, Amanda Heywood, Don
Last, Patrick McLeavey and Michael Michaels
Recipes: Alex Barker, Carla Capalbo, Frances Cleary, Carole Clements, Andi Clevely, Roz Denny, Nicola Diggins,
Stephanie Donaldson, Christine France, Silvana Franco, Sarah Gates, Shirley Gill, Patricia Lousada, Lesley Mackley,
Norma MacMillan, Sue Maggs, Sally Morris, Katherine Richmond, Liz Trigg, Hilaire Walden, Laura Washburn,
Steven Wheeler and Elizabeth Wolf-Cohen
Food for photography: Jacqueline Clark, Carole Handslip, Wendy Lee,
Lucie McKelvie, Jane Stevenson and Elizabeth Wolf-Cohen
Stylists: Madeleine Brehaut, Blake Minton, Kirsty Rawlings and Fiona Tillet

Previously printed as Mustard: A Book of Recipes
Printed and bound in Singapore

For all recipes, quantities are given in both metric and imperial measures and,
where appropriate, measures are also given in standard cups and spoons.
Follow one set, but not a mixture, because they are not interchangeable.

Contents

$\mathscr{I}$NTRODUCTION

$\mathbf{M}$ustard has had a place on the meal table for thousands of years. Wherever the plant grew, people discovered its pleasant fieriness and have either eaten the whole seeds or pounded them to make a condiment similar to today's prepared mustards. The Egyptians and Greeks were known to eat the whole seeds during meals, while the Romans used white mustard seeds to preserve their vegetables.

Mustard derives its name from the Italian word *mostarda*, which is the unfermented grape juice used originally, and is still used today with the better mustards, to blend the ground mustard seeds to a pulp.

In spite of the hundreds of mustards available in the shops, there are basically three types of mustard, which are made from the seeds of three varieties of the plant. Black mustard is the most prized, with a distinctive biting taste. Brown, or Indian mustard, though still pungent, is less intensely hot but with a more bitter initial flavour. Brown mustard seeds are used either by themselves in Dijon mustard or blended with other seeds for many of the prepared mustards.

The third type, white or yellow mustard, is native to the Mediterranean, but is now grown throughout Europe and North America. The honey-coloured seeds are a little larger than the black and brown seeds and have a generally milder taste. They are used extensively in American mustards and are also used in a variety of pickling spices.

While the seeds are the raw materials of the mustards we buy in the shops, a good mustard relies principally on the blending and macerating of the seeds. Mustard develops its pungent qualities once it is mixed with liquid. Mustard seeds, blended or used alone, are macerated in a liquid of unfermented grape juice, wine, vinegar, cider or water. As a rule, the better flavoured the liquid, the better the mustard. The list of ingredients on the jar tells you how the mustard is made. After they have been soaked, the seeds are ground to a fine paste and flavours can be added if required.

The heat of mustard is determined not only by the seeds but, more crucially, by the amount of seed husk that is sifted out. Stronger, hotter mustards contain less husk, while mild mustards, such as Bordeaux and Beaujolais, contain a higher percentage of the husk.

Mustard's distinct flavour is surprisingly versatile. The recipes in this book reveal how the clever use of mustard can create delicious dishes that range from soups and sauces, piquant curries and casseroles to delightful home-made pickles, chutneys and relishes.

TYPES OF MUSTARD

BLACK MUSTARD SEEDS (NIGRA)

These seeds have a distinctive and pungent flavour and are the hottest of all the mustard seeds. They are used for blended mustards, as well as whole in many Indian dishes, adding their own characteristic spiciness.

BROWN MUSTARD SEEDS (JUNCEA)

These do not have quite the intense pungency of black seeds but are distinctly piquant. They are the most commonly grown of the mustard seeds and are used extensively in Dijon mustards and blended in many English and French mustards, too.

WHITE OR YELLOW MUSTARD SEEDS (ALBA)

These large, sandy-brown seeds are native to the Mediterranean area and are less fiery than the black or brown seeds. They are frequently used in American prepared mustards and are also sometimes added to brown or black seeds for English mustards. These are the seeds grown with garden cress for mustard and cress and they are also widely used whole for pickling.

ENGLISH MUSTARD POWDER (DRY MUSTARD)

This fine, bright yellow powder is made from ground white and black or brown seeds mixed with a little flour and turmeric for bulk and colour. Like the seeds, mustard powder is bland when dry and acquires its heat only when water is added. Once blended, however, it is extremely robust and hot.

MUSTARD SEED OIL

This oil is obtained from brown mustard seeds. It is used in India as an alternative to ghee and adds a pleasant piquant flavour. Do not overheat, as its fiery properties will be driven off.

MUSTARD SEED SPROUTS

These are grown from white mustard seeds and are eaten in salads or used as a garnish. To grow your own, scatter about 30ml/2 tbsp seeds on a thin layer of soil in a small tray, on a piece of damp cloth, or in a muslin-covered jar. Keep the seeds moist and, if growing in a jar, rinse and drain once or twice a day. They will be ready to eat in about 2 weeks when about 5cm/2in high. To grow with cress, plant the cress seeds 3–4 days after the mustard seeds as they germinate more quickly.

Yellow

Brown

Black

Crushed yellow seeds

English mustard powder

Mustard seed sprouts

Mustard seed oil

$\mathscr{P}$REPARED $\mathscr{M}$USTARDS

FRENCH MUSTARDS

Dijon is the most famous of French mustards and the town is the mustard centre of the world, accounting for half of the world's production. The mustard was traditionally made from black seeds but is now made from husked brown seeds blended with verjuice (the sour juice from unripe grapes or wild apples), wine or vinegar, salt and spices. Most Dijons are creamy lemon in colour with a strong but subtle flavour, although some are mild and delicate. Bordeaux mustard (unhusked black and brown seeds blended with unfermented red wine) and Moutarde de Meaux (partly crushed, partly ground, black seeds, vinegar and spices) are also popular.

ENGLISH MUSTARDS

Traditional English mustards available in shops and supermarkets are ready-mixed dry mustards. Some of these mustards come flavoured with honey, horse-radish and chilli. In addition there are numerous locally produced mustards, mostly wholegrain, flavoured with a range of ingredients.

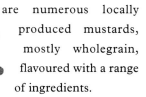

WHOLEGRAIN MUSTARDS

These are mild Dijon-style mustards that contain the whole seed that has been lightly crushed in order to release the volatile oils. Moutarde de Meaux is the most popular, though there are many others to choose from.

GERMAN MUSTARDS

These mustards are a blend of black mustard seeds and vinegar in a choice of strengths to suit different palates. *Senf* mustards are generally milder than English mustards, with aromatic overtones, but the *scharf* or *extra scharf* (hot or extra hot) can be very fiery indeed.

AMERICAN MUSTARDS

Traditional American mustards are made only from white (yellow) seeds, blended with sugar and wine or vinegar. They are bright yellow with a mild and sweet flavour and are slightly thinner than other mustards.

FLAVOURED MUSTARDS

There is really no limit to the ingredients that can be added to mustards and the result can be spectacular, both in flavour and appearance. Herbs and spices, tomatoes, horseradish, honey, beer and whisky are among the more common additions.

Dijon

Wholegrain

English

German

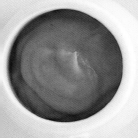

French

American

Honeycup

Herb and tomato

Whisky and leeks

ℬasic 𝒯echniques

COOKING WITH MUSTARD

To mix dry mustard, blend enough cold water with the powder (about 1.5ml/¼ tsp per person is sufficient) to make a smooth paste. The water should never be hot or the mustard will release bitter oils and spoil the taste. Made-up mustard should always be freshly made in small quantities; allow it to stand for about 15 minutes to develop the heat. For mild mustard, blend with milk, a little cream and a pinch of sugar. For a thick Tewskesbury mustard, blend the powder with wine vinegar or apple juice or use beer or claret.

STORING MUSTARD
- Prepared mustards will keep for up to one year, though they will gradually lose their strength once opened. If you don't use mustard frequently, buy small jars, rather than economy-sized ones, or the mustard will be past its best when it is finally all eaten. Keep in the fridge or a cool place.

- Made-up mustard should be prepared only in small quantities and used the same day.
- Store seeds in an airtight container and keep in a cool dry place for up to one year.

Mustard seeds should be fried briefly to bring out their flavour. Heat a little oil or ghee in a saucepan or small frying pan and add the seeds. Fry for 1–2 minutes, shaking the pan or stirring frequently, until the seeds start to change colour and begin to pop. Remove the pan from the heat and add to the recipe as required.

When frying whole mustard seeds, especially if using a shallow pan or frying pan, be prepared for the seeds to pop. A handy lid will prevent the seeds popping out of the pan.

PERFECT PARTNERS

Although valued as a cooking ingredient, mustard was, of course, originally used simply as an accompaniment, a role that it still performs with panache. Here is a brief guide to choosing the right mustard.

Dijon mustard: The ideal mustard for vinaigrettes and mayonnaise and for delicate sauces. It is also excellent eaten with steaks and grills and is probably the most indispensable of all the mustards.

Bordeaux mustard: Blended with vinegar and sugar, tarragon and other herbs and spices, this mustard has a mild, earthy, aromatic flavour which makes it superb with steak, cold meats and sausages.

Meaux mustard: Mixed with vinegar and spices, this medium to hot mustard is good with cold meats, meat pies or sausages.

English mustard: Made-up English mustard is particularly good with roast beef and with ham, pork, gammon and sausages. It is also a firm favourite with Cheddar cheese.

German mustard: Choose a fairly mild, coarse-grained mustard, which will complement most of the German sausages, unless you are partial to particularly strong mustard, in which case choose *extra scharf*.

American mustard: The obligatory accompaniment for the all-American hot dog and burger, it has a mild, sweet taste. It can also be used in mayonnaise, giving it a distinct flavour.

Wholegrain mustard: Best eaten with cold meats or cheeses, but flavoured wholegrains can be stirred into sauces. Honey-flavoured wholegrains are good with pork, while those blended with horseradish can be served with beef or added to stews and sauces.

Flavoured mustards: Mustards can be flavoured with the addition of herbs, spices or other ingredients. Choose a mild Dijon or wholegrain mustard, add your flavouring, and let it stand for at least 10 minutes before using.

Herbs – Add 10ml/2 tsp chopped fresh herbs. Choose from mint, basil, thyme, sage, tarragon and chervil. Use singly or mix together two or three herbs.

Spices – Add 2.5ml/½ tsp, such as whole or ground cumin and coriander, crushed green peppercorns, grated fresh root ginger and ground turmeric.

Other flavourings – There are many other suitable flavourings to choose from, such as honey, lemon, finely chopped chillies and horseradish.

MUSTARD SAUCES

As a rule, use prepared mustard for mustard sauces, particularly for dressings and mayonnaise. When making a dressing, whisk the mustard in at the beginning with the vinegar (or with the egg yolk for mayonnaise) to help the emulsification process. A little extra mustard can be stirred in at the end if necessary.

MAYONNAISE

Sunflower oil produces a lightly flavoured mayonnaise; olive oil gives a stronger, fruitier flavour. Or use half of each for a well-flavoured compromise.

Whisk or blend in a food processor 2 egg yolks, 15ml/1 tbsp Dijon mustard and a pinch of salt. Slowly add 300ml/½ pint/1¼ cups sunflower or olive oil, increasing the amount of oil as the mayonnaise thickens. When thick, stir in 15–30ml/1–2 tbsp white wine vinegar to thin the mixture, then continue adding the oil. Add a little more vinegar to taste and adjust seasoning.

GRAVADLAX

Blend together 30ml/2 tbsp mild Swedish or German mustard with 10ml/2 tsp caster sugar and 1 egg yolk. Gradually whisk in 150ml/ ¼ pint/⅔ cup sunflower oil drop by drop at first, until the sauce is thick. Add about 30ml/2 tbsp white wine vinegar and 30ml/2 tbsp chopped fresh dill. Mix well, cover and keep in a cool place for at least 24 hours to allow the flavours to blend.

MUSTARD SAUCE

Melt 25g/1oz/2 tbsp margarine or butter in a small pan, stir in 25g/ 1oz/3 tbsp plain flour and cook gently for 1 minute, stirring. Gradually stir in 300ml/½ pint/1¼ cups milk, bring to the boil and continue cooking, stirring all the time, until the sauce is bubbling. Stir in 15ml/1 tbsp prepared mustard and season with salt and pepper to taste. This makes a thick coating sauce.

For a pouring sauce, decrease the margarine or butter and plain flour or increase the amount of milk until you get the desired consistency.

SIMPLE IDEAS

• To make a classic French dressing, place 90ml/6 tbsp olive oil, 15ml/1 tbsp white wine vinegar, 10ml/ 2 tsp Dijon mustard and a pinch of sugar in a screw-top jar. Replace the lid and shake vigorously until the dressing has emulsified and is thick.

• Mustard seeds can be added to salad oils to enhance the flavour. Use brown or black seeds and roast briefly. Allow to cool and place in a pretty bottle with other spices, such as cardamom or coriander, if liked. Top up the bottle with a good-quality olive oil or a light sunflower oil.

• Mustard butter is surprisingly easy to make. Blend 10–15ml/2–3 tsp mustard into 115g/4oz/½ cup softened unsalted butter. Stand in a cool place for 1 hour to allow the flavours to develop and then chill. The butter can be rolled out between sheets of greaseproof paper and then cut into shapes, or simply rolled into balls. Choose a mustard which will suit the dish you intend to serve. A wholegrain mustard with tarragon or chives looks attractive and has a delicate piquancy. In general, choose among the milder and paler mustards for a subtle flavour and pretty appearance.

POTTED CHEESE RAREBIT

In this version of the classic rarebit, the cheese has been given extra bite using a well-flavoured French mustard.

Place 50g/2oz/4 tbsp butter, 15ml/1 tbsp French mustard, 2.5ml/½ tsp ground black pepper and 120ml/4 fl oz/½ cup pale ale or cider in a saucepan and heat gently, stirring occasionally, until boiling. Remove from the heat and add 450g/1lb mature Cheddar cheese, grated, stirring until the cheese has melted and the mixture is creamy. Pour into pretty sterilized pots, cover and leave until cold. Chill to set and then label. Keep in a cool place and use within 4 weeks. If the cheese and ale separate or the cheese doesn't completely melt, blend 15ml/1 tbsp cornflour with a little cold water and stir into the mixture. Place over a very gentle heat. Makes 675g/1½lb.

Starters and Snacks

It is easy to liven up all sorts of starters with a
dash of mustard. Stir it into soups or creamy
sauces or combine with everyday ingredients
for a devilishly-spiced result.

CREAMY PARSNIP AND MUSTARD SOUP

This delicate, lightly spiced soup is given a special touch with a pretty and aromatic garnish of garlic and yellow-coloured mustard seeds.

Serves 4–6

40g/1 1/2oz/3 tbsp butter
1 onion, chopped
675g/1 1/2lb parsnips, diced
5ml/1 tsp ground coriander
2.5ml/1/2 tsp ground cumin
2.5ml/1/2 tsp ground turmeric
1.5ml/1/4 tsp chilli powder
1.2 litres/2 pints/5 cups chicken stock
150ml/1/4 pint/2/3 cup single cream
15ml/1 tbsp sunflower oil
1 garlic clove, cut into julienne strips
10ml/2 tsp white mustard seeds
salt and ground black pepper

Melt the butter in a large pan and gently fry the onion and parsnip for 2–3 minutes. Stir in the spices, cook for a further 1 minute and add the chicken stock. Season with salt and pepper, bring to the boil and then simmer, covered, for about 45 minutes until the parsnips are tender.

Cool slightly and purée the soup in a blender until smooth. Return the soup to the pan, add the cream and heat through gently over a low heat.

Heat the oil in a small pan and briefly fry the garlic and mustard seeds until the garlic begins to brown and the mustard seeds start to pop. Remove the pan from the heat. Ladle the soup into warmed bowls and sprinkle a little of the hot mustard and garlic over the top. Serve at once.

DIJON DEVILLED EGGS

Devilled food is seasoned with spicy ingredients, and almost always includes mustard. Dijon mustard, with its strong and distinct flavour, is an excellent foil to eggs.

Serves 6

6 hard-boiled eggs, shelled

25g/1oz/¼ cup cooked ham, very finely chopped or minced

6 walnut halves, very finely chopped

1 spring onion, very finely chopped

15ml/1 tbsp Dijon mustard

15ml/1 tbsp mayonnaise

10ml/2 tsp white wine vinegar

1.5ml/¼ tsp salt

1.5ml/¼ tsp ground black pepper

1.5ml/¼ tsp cayenne pepper (optional)

paprika and a few slices of dill pickle, to garnish

COOK'S TIP

If making eggs for a buffet party, serve with celery sticks, stuffed with a blend of blue cheese, cream cheese and a good pinch of dry mustard.

Cut each egg in half lengthways, remove the yolks and place them in a bowl. Set the egg whites aside.

Mash the yolks thoroughly with a fork and then add the ham, walnuts, spring onion, mustard, mayonnaise, vinegar, salt and pepper and cayenne pepper, if using. Stir thoroughly to mix and adjust the seasoning to taste.

Spoon the filling into the egg white halves and garnish the top of each egg with a little paprika and a small slice of dill pickle. Serve the stuffed eggs at room temperature.

POTATO KEBABS WITH MUSTARD DIP

These charcoal-baked, crispy-skinned potatoes, partnered with tender shallots, are quite delicious, especially with the spicy mustard mayonnaise.

Serves 4

900g/2lb small new potatoes
200g/7oz/2 cups shallots, halved
30ml/2 tbsp olive oil
15ml/1 tbsp sea salt

For the mustard dip
4 garlic cloves, crushed
2 egg yolks
30ml/2 tbsp lemon juice
300ml/¹/₂ pint/1¹/₄ cups olive oil
10ml/2 tsp wholegrain mustard
salt and ground black pepper

COOK'S TIP
For a successful mayonnaise, make sure that the egg yolks are at room temperature.

First make the dip. Place the garlic, egg yolks and lemon juice in a blender or food processor and process for a few seconds until smooth. Keep the motor running and gradually add the oil, pouring it in a thin stream until the mixture forms a thick glossy cream. Add the mustard and season with salt and pepper.

Par-boil the potatoes for 5 minutes, drain well and then thread them on to metal skewers, alternating with the shallots. Preheat a barbecue or grill. Brush the potatoes thoroughly with olive oil and sprinkle with sea salt. Cook for 10–12 minutes over hot coals or under the grill until completely tender, turning occasionally. Serve with the mustard dip.

CRISPY CELERIAC WITH MUSTARD DIP

The rather unattractive appearance of celeriac with its hard, knobbly skin, belies a deliciously sweet, nutty flavour. The combination here of hot, crispy celeriac fritters and cold mustard sauce is a perfect match.

Serves 4

1 egg
115g/4oz/1 cup ground almonds
45ml/3 tbsp freshly grated Parmesan
  cheese
45ml/3 tbsp chopped fresh parsley
1 medium celeriac, about 450g/1lb
lemon juice
sunflower oil, for deep-frying
salt and ground black pepper
sea salt flakes, for sprinkling

For the mustard sauce
150ml/¼ pint/⅔ cup soured cream
15–30ml/1–2 tbsp wholegrain
  mustard

To make the mustard sauce, place the soured cream in a small bowl and stir in the mustard and a little salt. Cover and chill until ready to serve.

Beat the egg well and pour into a shallow dish. Mix the almonds, grated Parmesan cheese and parsley in a separate shallow dish and season with salt and plenty of pepper. Set aside. Peel the celeriac and cut into strips about 1cm/½in wide and 5cm/2in long. Drop them immediately into a bowl of water with a little lemon juice added to prevent discoloration.

Heat the oil to 180°C/350°F in a deep fryer. Drain and pat dry half the celeriac chips and dip them first into the beaten egg and then into the ground almond mixture. Deep fry, a few at a time, for 2–3 minutes until golden. Drain and keep warm while you cook the rest. Sprinkle with sea salt flakes and serve at once with the mustard sauce.

COOK'S TIP
The sauce can be made in advance and kept cool, but the fritters should be cooked and served immediately.

MUSTARD, APPLE AND CHEESE TART

A little mustard is used in both the pastry and the filling of this delicious French tart, bringing out the flavour of the apples and onion.

Serves 4–6

225g/8oz/2 cups plain flour
1.5ml/¼ tsp dry mustard
75g/3oz/6 tbsp soft margarine
75g/3oz/6 tbsp Gruyère, grated

For the filling
25g/1oz/2 tbsp butter
1 large onion, finely chopped
1 large or 2 small eating apples,
  peeled and grated
2 large eggs
150ml/¼ pint/⅔ cup double cream
1.5ml/¼ tsp mixed herbs
1.5ml/¼ tsp dry mustard
115g/4oz Gruyère cheese
salt and ground black pepper
mixed salad leaves, to garnish

COOK'S TIP
This recipe is equally delicious with other hard cheeses, such as Red Leicester or Cheddar.

First make the pastry: sift the flour, a pinch of salt and the dry mustard into a bowl. Rub in the margarine and cheese until the mixture resembles soft breadcrumbs. Add 30ml/2 tbsp cold water and stir with a knife to form a ball. Knead lightly and then chill, covered for 30 minutes.

Meanwhile, make the filling: melt the butter in a frying pan and fry the onion over a gentle heat for 10 minutes until softened but not browned, stirring occasionally. Stir in the grated apples and cook for 2–3 minutes. Set aside to cool.

Roll out the pastry and line a greased 20cm/8in springform tin. Chill for 20 minutes. Preheat the oven to 200°C/400°F/Gas 6. Line the pastry with greaseproof paper and fill with baking beans. Bake blind for 20 minutes.

Beat together the eggs, cream, herbs, mustard and seasoning. Grate three-quarters of the cheese and stir into the egg mixture, then slice the remaining cheese and set aside. When the pastry is part-cooked, remove the beans and paper and pour in the egg mixture.

Arrange the sliced cheese over the top. Reduce the oven temperature to 190°C/375°F/Gas 5 and cook the tart for 20 minutes until the filling is golden and just firm. Serve hot or warm, garnished with a few salad leaves.

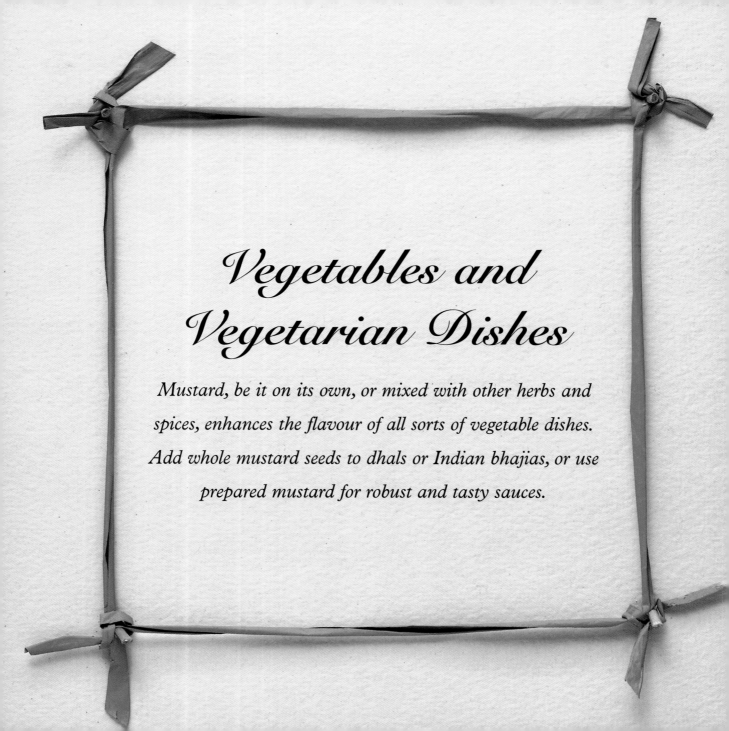

Vegetables and Vegetarian Dishes

Mustard, be it on its own, or mixed with other herbs and spices, enhances the flavour of all sorts of vegetable dishes. Add whole mustard seeds to dhals or Indian bhajias, or use prepared mustard for robust and tasty sauces.

LEEKS WITH MUSTARD DRESSING

The mustard dressing transforms these tender sweet leeks into an unusual and delicious salad.

Serves 4

8 slim leeks

5–10ml/1–2 tsp Dijon mustard

10ml/2 tsp white wine vinegar

1 hard-boiled egg, halved lengthways
and separated

75ml/5 tbsp olive oil

10ml/2 tsp chopped fresh parsley

salt and ground black pepper

COOK'S TIP

Although this dish is served
cold, make sure the leeks are still
warm when you pour over the
dressing, so that they absorb the
mustardy flavour.

Steam the leeks over a pan of boiling water until just tender. Place the mustard and vinegar in a bowl and add the egg yolk. Mash thoroughly with a fork and then gradually whisk in the oil to make a smooth sauce. Season to taste with salt and pepper.

Lift the leeks out of the steamer and drain on several layers of kitchen paper. Cover with several more layers of kitchen paper and pat dry.

Transfer the leeks to a serving dish, spoon the dressing over them and leave to cool. Finely chop the egg white and mix with the parsley. Sprinkle over the leeks and chill until ready to serve.

CHEESE AND MUSTARD FRICASSEE

The tangy mustard sauce brings out the flavour of the courgettes, beans and tomatoes in this simple but tasty vegetarian dish.

Serves 4

4 courgettes, sliced
115g/4oz green beans, sliced
4 large tomatoes, skinned and sliced
50g/2oz/4 tbsp butter
1 onion, sliced
40g/1 1/2oz/1/3 cup plain flour
10ml/2 tsp wholegrain mustard
450ml/3/4 pint/2 cups milk
150ml/1/4 pint/2/3 cup natural yogurt
5ml/1 tsp dried thyme
115g/4oz/1 cup mature Cheddar
*   cheese, grated*
60ml/4 tbsp fresh wholemeal
*   breadcrumbs, tossed with*
*   15ml/1 tbsp sunflower oil*
salt and ground black pepper

Blanch the courgettes and beans in a little boiling water for 5 minutes and then drain and arrange in a shallow ovenproof dish. Arrange all but three slices of the tomatoes on top.

Melt the butter in a small saucepan and fry the onion over a gentle heat for 4–5 minutes until soft but not browned. Stir in the flour and the mustard, cook for 1 minute and then gradually add the milk to make a smooth sauce. Simmer for a further 2 minutes.

Reduce the heat and stir in the yogurt, thyme and cheese, taking care not to allow the sauce to boil or the yogurt will curdle. Season to taste with salt and pepper.

Pour the sauce over the vegetables and scatter the breadcrumbs on top. Brown under a preheated grill until golden and crisp, taking care that the breadcrumbs do not burn. Garnish with the reserved tomato slices and serve.

COOK'S TIP
If liked, serve with a crusty Italian bread and a green salad.

Glazed Carrots with Mustard

The lovely sharpness of the Dijon mustard, combined with the cider, turns the humble carrot into a delicious and elegant dish, worthy of any dinner party.

Serves 4

450g/1lb young carrots

25g/1oz/2 tbsp butter

15ml/1 tbsp brown sugar

120ml/4fl oz/½ cup dry or
    medium-dry cider

60ml/4 tbsp vegetable stock or water

5ml/1 tsp Dijon mustard

15ml/1 tbsp finely chopped
    fresh parsley

Cook's tip

If the carrots cook before the liquid in the pan has reduced, transfer to a serving dish and boil the liquid in the pan until thick. Pour over the carrots and sprinkle the parsley on top.

Scrape the carrots and cut into julienne strips. Melt the butter in a saucepan, add the carrots and sauté for 4–5 minutes, stirring frequently. Sprinkle over the sugar and cook, stirring, for a further 1 minute or until the sugar has dissolved.

Add the cider and vegetable stock or water, bring to the boil and stir in the mustard. Partially cover the pan and simmer for 10–12 minutes until the carrots are almost tender, then remove the lid and continue cooking so that the liquid is reduced to a thick sauce. Remove from the heat, stir in the parsley and then spoon into a warmed serving dish.

BOMBAY SPICY POTATOES

This popular Indian dish uses a mixture of whole and ground spices. The brown mustard seeds have a slightly piquant flavour which perfectly complements the mellow pungency of the cumin and coriander.

Serves 4

4 large potatoes, cubed
60ml/4 tbsp sunflower oil
1 garlic clove, finely chopped
10ml/2 tsp brown mustard seeds
5ml/1 tsp black onion seeds
   (optional)
5ml/1 tsp ground turmeric
5ml/1 tsp ground cumin
5ml/1 tsp ground coriander
5ml/1 tsp fennel seeds
lemon juice
salt and ground black pepper
chopped fresh coriander and lemon
   wedges, to garnish

COOK'S TIP
Brown mustard seeds and black onion seeds are available from most large health food stores and Indian grocers.

Boil the potatoes in plenty of salted water for about 4 minutes until just tender. Drain well.

Heat the oil in a large frying pan, add the garlic and all the whole and ground spices and fry gently, stirring, for 1–2 minutes, until the mustard seeds start to pop. Add the potatoes and stir-fry over a moderate heat for about 5 minutes until heated through and thoroughly coated in the spicy oil.

Season with salt and pepper and sprinkle with a good squeeze of lemon juice. Serve garnished with the chopped coriander and lemon wedges.

Black Mustard and Ginger Dhal

Whole mustard seeds are a favourite ingredient in Indian cookery, especially in dhals, where their gentle heat contrasts well with the soft mellow lentils.

Serves 4–6

225g/8oz/1 cup yellow split peas
2 onions, chopped
1 large bay leaf
600ml/1 pint/2½ cups vegetable
  stock or water
25g/1oz/2 tbsp butter
10ml/2 tsp brown or black mustard
  seeds
1 garlic clove, crushed
2.5cm/1in cube fresh root ginger,
  grated
1 small green pepper, seeded
  and sliced
5ml/1 tsp ground turmeric
5ml/1 tsp garam masala or mild
  curry powder
3 tomatoes, skinned and chopped
salt and ground black pepper
fresh coriander or flat-leaf parsley,
  to garnish
Indian bread, to serve

Place the split peas, one of the chopped onions and the bay leaf in a saucepan, add the stock or water and bring to the boil. Cover and simmer over a gentle heat for 25 minutes until the peas are tender, adding a little more water if necessary. Season with salt and pepper.

Meanwhile, melt the butter in a large frying pan and fry the mustard seeds for about 30 seconds until they begin to pop. Add the other onion along with the garlic, ginger and green pepper and fry gently for about 5 minutes until the onion and pepper have softened. Stir in the turmeric and garam masala or curry powder and fry for a few seconds more.

Add the split peas and any cooking liquid, the tomatoes and a little extra water if necessary. Cover and simmer for 10 minutes until the peas are very soft and the flavours have combined. Adjust the seasoning, garnish with coriander or parsley and serve with warm Indian bread.

INDIAN RICE WITH MUSTARD SEEDS

Whole mustard seeds, combined with other spices and nuts, give this Indian dish a wonderful flavour.

Serves 4–6

225g/8oz/1¼ cups basmati rice

15–30ml/1–2 tbsp sunflower oil

1 onion, chopped

1 garlic clove, crushed

1 large carrot, coarsely grated

5ml/1 tsp cumin seeds

10ml/2 tsp ground coriander

10ml/2 tsp brown or black mustard
   seeds

4 cardamom pods

450ml/¾ pint/2 cups vegetable stock
   or water

1 bay leaf

75g/3oz/½ cup unsalted nuts,
   such as cashews, almonds
   and pistachios

salt and ground black pepper

chopped fresh parsley or coriander,
   to garnish

Rinse the rice in cold water and drain in a sieve. Heat the oil in a large frying pan and fry the onion, garlic and carrot for 2–3 minutes. Add the rice, cumin, coriander, mustard seeds and cardamom pods and cook for a further minute, stirring all the time to coat the grains in oil.

Pour in the stock or water and add the bay leaf. Season well, bring to the boil and then cover and simmer very gently for about 10 minutes. Remove from the heat, without lifting the lid, and leave for about 5 minutes. (This helps the rice firm up and cook further.)

Discard the bay leaf and cardamom pods and stir in the nuts. Scatter the rice with chopped parsley or coriander and serve.

MUSTARDY GLAMORGAN SAUSAGES

These vegetarian sausages are given bite by using a spicy wholegrain mustard.

Serves 4

*115g/4oz/2 cups fresh wholemeal
   breadcrumbs*

*175g/6oz/1 ½ cups mature Cheddar
   or Caerphilly cheese, grated*

*30ml/2 tbsp finely chopped leek or
   spring onion*

30ml/2 tbsp chopped fresh parsley

15ml/1 tbsp chopped fresh marjoram

15ml/1 tbsp wholegrain mustard

2 eggs, 1 separated

40g/1 ½ oz/½ cup dried breadcrumbs

oil, for deep frying

ground black pepper

*mashed potatoes and buttered
   cabbage, to serve*

COOK'S TIP

*The mixture will appear dry at
first, but knead it lightly with
your fingers and it will soon
come together.*

Mix the fresh breadcrumbs with the cheese, leek or onion, parsley, marjoram and mustard. Add 1 whole egg and the yolk of the other egg, season with pepper and mix thoroughly. Divide the mixture into eight and form into small sausages.

Whisk the egg white until lightly frothy and place the dried breadcrumbs on a shallow plate. Dip the sausages first into the egg white and then into the breadcrumbs, shaking off any excess.

Heat the oil in a deep fryer and fry the sausages, four at a time, for about 2 minutes each until golden. Drain on kitchen paper and keep warm while cooking the rest. Serve hot with mashed potatoes and buttered cabbage.

Meat and Poultry

Hot English mustard and strong but mellow Dijon
mustard are known favourites with meat dishes. Chicken,
too, is enhanced by a mild but spicy mustard, or choose a
delicately flavoured wholegrain, which complements
all sorts of meat dishes.

RACK OF LAMB WITH MUSTARD

Dijon mustard has a distinctive flavour that is the perfect complement to the meat in this French dish.

Serves 6–8

2–3 garlic cloves

115g/4oz/2 cups fresh white or
   wholemeal breadcrumbs

25ml/1 ½ tbsp fresh thyme leaves or
   15ml/1 tbsp rosemary leaves

25ml/1 ½ tbsp Dijon mustard

30ml/2 tbsp olive oil

3 racks of lamb (7–8 ribs each),
   trimmed of fat (see Cook's Tip)

ground black pepper

fresh rosemary, to garnish

lightly cooked broccoli and
   cauliflower, to serve

COOK'S TIP

*Ask your butcher to chine and
trim the racks of lamb. Trim any
remaining fat from the lamb,
including the fat over the meat.*

Preheat the oven to 220°C/425°F/Gas 7. Place the garlic cloves in a food processor and process until finely chopped, then add the breadcrumbs, thyme or rosemary, mustard and a little pepper and process until combined. Slowly pour in the oil to make a smooth mixture.

Press the stuffing on to the meaty side and ends of the lamb, patting down well to cover the surface completely.

Place the racks in a shallow roasting tin and cook in the oven for about 25 minutes for medium-rare or 35 minutes for medium. Transfer the racks to a carving board or warmed serving plate. Cut carefully down between the bones to separate them into chops, then serve garnished with rosemary and accompanied by lightly cooked broccoli and cauliflower.

BEEF WITH ORANGE HERB MUSTARD

An orange herb mustard is delicious with many different dishes, including cold ham and pork pies. It gives beef a fantastic flavour and will become a firm favourite.

Serves 4

2 oranges

45ml/3 tbsp sunflower oil

675g/1¹/₂lb braising steak, cubed

2 onions, chopped

1 garlic clove, crushed

30ml/2 tbsp plain flour

300ml/¹/₂ pint/1¹/₄ cups beef stock

15ml/1 tbsp tomato purée

45ml/3 tbsp Grand Marnier or other
  orange liqueur

15ml/1 tbsp maple syrup

115g/4oz/1¹/₂ cups button
  mushrooms, sliced

salt and ground black pepper

orange slices, to garnish

mashed potatoes, to serve

For the orange herb mustard

juice and grated rind of ¹/₂ orange

30ml/2 tbsp finely chopped fresh
  herbs, such as thyme, chives
  and parsley

45ml/3 tbsp Dijon mustard

First make the orange herb mustard: mix the orange rind with the herbs and then blend in the orange juice and Dijon mustard. Place in a small serving dish and set aside.

Prepare the oranges by cutting away the coloured part of the rind and slicing this into small pieces. Squeeze the juice of both oranges and set aside. Preheat the oven to 180°C/350°F/Gas 4.

Heat the oil in a large flameproof casserole and fry the beef until evenly browned. Transfer with a slotted spoon to a plate. Add the onions and garlic to the casserole and gently fry for 3–4 minutes until slightly softened. Transfer to the plate holding the meat and stir the flour into the pan. Cook for 1 minute and then gradually add the beef stock and cook, stirring to make a smooth sauce.

Add the tomato purée, Grand Marnier or other orange liqueur, maple syrup and the orange rind and juice, stir well and then stir in the meat and onions, together with any accumulated juices. Cook in the oven for about 1¹/₂ hours until the meat is tender. Add the mushrooms and return to the oven for a further 30 minutes. Spoon the beef on to warmed plates and garnish with slices of orange. Serve with mashed potatoes and with the orange herb mustard.

VENISON WITH MUSTARD DUMPLINGS

Mustard, juniper berries and bay leaves combine with lean dark venison to create a casserole with a rich flavour and a wonderful aroma.

Serves 6

about 15ml/1 tbsp olive oil

675g/1 ¹/₂lb stewing venison, cut into cubes

3 onions, sliced

2 garlic cloves, crushed

15ml/1 tbsp plain flour

5ml/1 tsp dry mustard

6 juniper berries, lightly crushed

2 bay leaves

400ml/14fl oz/1 ²/₃ cups Guinness

10ml/2 tsp soft light brown sugar

30ml/2 tbsp balsamic vinegar

salt and ground black pepper

For the mustard dumplings

175g/6oz/1 ¹/₂ cups self-raising flour

5ml/1 tsp dry English mustard

75g/3oz/generous ¹/₂ cup shredded beef suet

10ml/2 tsp horseradish sauce

Preheat the oven to 180°C/350°F/Gas 4. Heat the oil in a flameproof casserole and fry the meat, a few pieces at a time, until evenly browned. Transfer the meat to a plate and add the onions to the casserole, plus a little more oil, if necessary. Cook, stirring, for 5–6 minutes until soft, then add the garlic and return the venison.

Blend the flour and mustard in a small bowl and sprinkle over the meat. Stir well until the flour has been absorbed, then add the juniper berries and bay leaves and gradually stir in the Guinness, sugar and vinegar. Pour over enough water to cover the meat, season with salt and pepper and bring to simmering point. Cover and cook in the oven for 2–2¹/₂ hours until the meat is tender, stirring occasionally and adding a little water if necessary.

About 20 minutes before the end of the cooking time, make the dumplings. Mix the flour, mustard and a little seasoning in a bowl and stir in the suet. Add the horseradish sauce and enough water to make a soft dough. With floured hands, form into six dumplings and place these gently on top of the venison. Cover again and cook for 15 minutes until the dumplings are well risen and cooked. Serve at once.

STIR-FRIED PORK WITH MUSTARD

This is a wonderfully simple dish with all the flavours of Normandy – apples, Calvados and mustard.

Serves 4

500g/1 1/4 lb pork fillet

1 tart eating apple, such as Granny
 Smith

40g/1 1/2oz/3 tbsp unsalted butter

15ml/1 tbsp caster sugar

1 small onion, finely chopped

30ml/2 tbsp Calvados

15ml/1 tbsp Meaux or wholegrain
 mustard

150ml/1/4 pint/2/3 cup double cream

30ml/2 tbsp chopped fresh parsley

flat-leaf parsley sprigs, to garnish

COOK'S TIP
*Fry the apples very carefully, as
they will disintegrate if they are
overcooked.*

Cut the pork into thin slices; peel, core and thickly slice the apple. Melt half the butter in a large frying pan or wok and add the apple slices. Sprinkle with sugar and stir-fry for 2–3 minutes. Transfer the apple to a plate and wipe the pan with kitchen paper.

Melt the remaining butter in the pan and stir-fry the pork and onion for 2–3 minutes until the pork is golden and the onion has begun to soften. Stir in the Calvados and boil until it has reduced by half. Stir in the mustard and add the cream and apples. Simmer over a low heat without boiling for about 1 minute, then stir in the parsley. Serve garnished with sprigs of flat-leaf parsley.

RABBIT WITH THREE MUSTARDS

This recipe combines three different mustards that each add their own distinctive flavour to the dish.

Serves 4

15ml/1 tbsp Dijon mustard

15ml/1 tbsp tarragon mustard

15ml/1 tbsp wholegrain mustard

1.5kg/3–3¹/₂lb rabbit portions

1 large carrot, sliced

1 onion, sliced

30ml/2 tbsp chopped fresh tarragon

120ml/4fl oz/¹/₂ cup dry white wine

150ml/¹/₄ pint/²/₃ cup double cream

salt and ground black pepper

sprig of fresh tarragon, to garnish

COOK'S TIP

If you do not have three different mustards, use one or two varieties, increasing the quantities accordingly. The flavour will not be quite as interesting, but the dish will still taste good.

Preheat the oven to 200°C/400°F/Gas 6. Mix the mustards in a bowl and spread over the rabbit. Place the carrot and onion slices in a roasting tin and scatter the chopped tarragon over them. Pour in 120ml/4fl oz/¹/₂ cup water, then arrange the meat on top.

Roast the rabbit for 25–30 minutes until tender, basting frequently with the juices from the tin. Transfer the rabbit to a heated serving dish and keep warm. Remove the carrot and onion slices from the roasting tin and discard.

Place the roasting tin on the hob and add the white wine. Bring to the boil, stirring all the time, and then boil until reduced by about two-thirds. Stir in the cream and allow to bubble for a few minutes. Season to taste and pour over the rabbit. Serve garnished with fresh tarragon.

KIDNEYS IN MUSTARD SAUCE

This sauce has a pleasantly strong mustard flavour that contrasts well with the kidneys. In France, veal kidneys are considered best, but lamb kidneys work equally well.

Serves 4

2 veal kidneys or 8–10 lamb kidneys,
   trimmed and membranes removed

15ml/1 tbsp sunflower oil

25g/1oz/2 tbsp butter

115g/4oz/1/2 cup button mushrooms,
   quartered

60ml/4 tbsp chicken stock

30ml/2 tbsp brandy (optional)

60ml/4 tbsp crème fraîche or
   soured cream

30ml/2 tbsp Dijon or American
   mustard

salt and ground black pepper

snipped fresh chives, to garnish

Cut the veal kidneys into pieces, discarding any fat. If using lamb kidneys, remove the central core by cutting a V-shape from the middle of each kidney. Cut each kidney into three or four pieces. Heat the oil and butter in a large frying pan over a high heat and fry the kidneys for 3–4 minutes until well browned, stirring frequently. Transfer to a plate with a slotted spoon.

Add the mushrooms and fry for 2–3 minutes until golden, stirring frequently. Pour in the chicken stock and brandy, if using, bring to the boil and cook for 2 minutes.

Stir in the crème fraîche or soured cream and simmer for a further 2–3 minutes until the sauce is slightly thickened. Add the mustard and season with salt and pepper, then add the kidneys and cook for 1 minute to reheat. Scatter over the chives before serving.

COOK'S TIP
Take care not to cook the sauce for too long once the mustard has been added, or the subtle flavour and piquancy of the mustard will be lost.

DIJON CHICKEN SALAD

The Dijon mustard in the marinade and in the honey-sweet dressing adds a wonderful burst of flavour to this elegant summery chicken salad.

Serves 4

4 boned and skinned chicken breasts
mixed salad leaves, e.g. frisée and
* oakleaf lettuce or radicchio, to serve*

For the mustard marinade
30ml/2 tbsp Dijon mustard
3 garlic cloves, crushed
15ml/1 tbsp grated onion
60ml/4 tbsp white wine

For the mustard dressing
30ml/2 tbsp tarragon wine vinegar
5ml/1 tsp Dijon mustard
5ml/1 tsp clear honey
90ml/6 tbsp olive oil
salt and ground black pepper

Mix all the marinade ingredients together in a large shallow dish and add the chicken breasts, turning them over in the marinade to coat evenly. Cover with clear film and chill in the fridge overnight.

Preheat the oven to 190°C/375°F/Gas 5. Transfer the chicken and marinade to an ovenproof dish, cover with foil and bake for about 35 minutes until tender. Leave to cool in the liquid.

To make the dressing, place the vinegar, mustard, honey, oil and seasoning in a screw-top jar and shake vigorously until well blended. Slice the chicken thinly and fan out the slices on a serving dish with the salad leaves. Spoon over some of the mustard dressing and serve.

MUSTARD AND TOMATO CHICKEN

The spicy mustard sauce gives a great barbecue flavour to these chicken pieces. They are equally good cooked in the oven or over a barbecue, so are a treat at any time of the year.

Serves 4

45ml/3 tbsp sunflower oil

1 large onion, chopped

175ml/6fl oz/³/₄ cup tomato ketchup

40ml/2¹/₂ tbsp fresh lemon juice

25ml/1¹/₂ tbsp grated horseradish

15ml/1 tbsp light brown sugar

15ml/1 tbsp French mustard

1.5kg/3–3¹/₂lb chicken pieces, either
    drumsticks, thighs, wings or breast
    portions

boiled or fried rice, to serve

COOK'S TIP
This sauce is excellent with all sorts of barbecued food; try it with sausages, lamb chops or pork kebabs.

Heat 15ml/1 tbsp of the oil in a pan and fry the onion for 4–5 minutes until softened but not brown. Stir in the ketchup, lemon juice, horseradish, brown sugar, mustard and 175ml/6fl oz/³/₄ cup water and bring to the boil. Reduce the heat and simmer for 10 minutes, stirring occasionally.

Preheat the oven to 180°C/350°F/Gas 4. Heat the remaining oil in a separate heavy frying pan and brown the chicken on all sides. Drain on kitchen paper and then place the chicken pieces in a roasting tin or ovenproof dish and pour the sauce over the top. Bake in the oven for about 1¹/₄ hours, basting occasionally. Alternatively, barbecue over a medium heat for 40–50 minutes, turning once and brushing frequently with the sauce.

Fish and Seafood

Fish is superb cooked or served with mustard.
Full-flavoured fish like herrings can be served with a
robust English mustard, while delicately flavoured white
fish is complemented by mild prepared or
wholegrain mustards.

LEMONY MUSTARD MACKEREL

Mustard is a classic accompaniment to oily fish like mackerel. English mustard is the traditional choice, though a plain or flavoured wholegrain mustard, as shown here, is just as tasty.

Serves 4

4 fresh mackerel, about 275g/10oz
*   each, cleaned and boned*
salt and ground black pepper
175–225g/6–8oz young spinach
*   leaves, to serve*

For the mustard and lemon butter

115g/4oz/½ cup butter, melted
30ml/2 tbsp wholegrain mustard
grated rind of 1 lemon
30ml/2 tbsp lemon juice
45ml/3 tbsp chopped fresh parsley

COOK'S TIP

To bone the fish, open it out skin side up and press down with the heel of your hand to loosen the backbone. Turn the fish over and lift away the backbone in one piece. Pick out any other loose bones.

Score the fish three or four times through the skin on each side and season inside and out with salt and pepper.

To make the mustard and lemon butter, mix together the melted butter, mustard, lemon rind and juice, parsley and seasoning. Place the mackerel on a grill, brush with a little of the mustard butter and grill for 5 minutes each side, basting occasionally with the mustard butter, until cooked through.

Arrange the spinach leaves in the centre of four large plates and place the mackerel on top. Heat the remaining mustard butter in a small pan until sizzling and pour over the mackerel. Serve at once.

COD WITH POTATO AND MUSTARD

The whole mustard seeds give extra bite to this delicious tapas-style Spanish dish.

Serves 2

30ml/2 tbsp olive oil

5ml/1 tsp mustard seeds

1 large potato, cubed

2 slices Serrano ham, shredded

1 onion, thinly sliced

2 garlic cloves, thinly sliced

1 red chilli, seeded and sliced

*115g/4oz skinned cod fillet, cut into
    small cubes*

120ml/4fl oz/¹/₂ cup vegetable stock

*50g/2oz/¹/₂ cup Cheddar cheese,
    grated*

salt and ground black pepper

COOK'S TIP

*Serrano is a well-known
Spanish ham from the
mountains around Granada.
If it is not available, use a dried
Italian ham or finely chopped
streaky bacon.*

Heat the oil in a heavy-based frying pan and add the mustard seeds. Fry for 1–2 minutes until they begin to pop, then add the potato, ham and onion. Cook for 10–15 minutes until the potato is golden brown and almost tender, stirring frequently. Add the garlic and chilli and cook gently for a further 2 minutes.

Stir in the fish cubes and cook for 2–3 minutes until the fish turns white, then add the stock and season well with salt and pepper. Cover and cook for 5 minutes until the fish is cooked and the potatoes are tender.

Transfer the mixture to a flameproof dish or pan and sprinkle over the grated cheese. Place the dish under a hot grill for 2–3 minutes until the cheese is golden and bubbling. Serve at once.

GRAVADLAX TROUT WITH MUSTARD

A tasty alternative to the classic gravadlax using trout, instead of salmon, with a piquant mustard sauce.

Serves 4
2 large trout, cleaned and with
heads removed
1 bunch dill

For the marinade (for each
450g/1lb of fish)
7.5ml/¹/₂ tbsp coarse sea salt
7.5ml/¹/₂ tbsp caster sugar
7.5ml/¹/₂ tbsp crushed peppercorns

For the mustard sauce
10ml/2 tsp German or
Swedish mustard
15ml/1 tbsp chopped fresh dill
10ml/2 tsp caster sugar
5ml/1 tsp cider vinegar
75ml/5 tbsp soured cream

Slit the trout along the belly, open it out skin side up and press firmly along the backbone down to the tail. Turn the fish over and carefully lift away the backbone in one piece. Pick out any other loose bones.

Place one fish, skin side down in a tight-fitting, non-metallic dish and lay the dill on top. Mix the marinade ingredients together and sprinkle evenly over the dill. Top with the other fish, cover with foil and place weights evenly on top of the fish. Chill for 48 hours, turning the fish every 6–12 hours and basting with the marinating ingredients.

Mix together the mustard sauce ingredients and chill. Scrape away the dill and pepper from the fish and pat dry. Cut into fillets or thinly slice the fish horizontally. Serve with the mustard sauce, garnished with dill sprigs.

Herrings in Oatmeal with Mustard

Crispy, oatmeal-covered herrings contrast perfectly with this cool and tangy mustard mayonnaise.

Serves 4

4 herrings, cleaned, with heads removed, about 225g/8oz each
juice of 1 lemon
115g/4oz/1 cup medium oatmeal
salt and ground black pepper
green beans, to serve

For the mustard sauce
175ml/6fl oz/³⁄₄ cup thick mayonnaise
15ml/1 tbsp Dijon or German mustard
about 7.5ml/¹⁄₂ tbsp tarragon vinegar

To make the mustard sauce, mix the mayonnaise with the mustard and enough vinegar to produce a tangy dressing. Chill.

To bone the fish, place it skin side up on a board and press gently along the backbone. Turn the fish over and lift away the backbone in one piece. Pick out any other loose bones. Squeeze a little lemon juice over both sides of the fish and season with salt and pepper. Reshape the fish, skin side outwards.

Preheat a grill until fairly hot. Place the oatmeal on a plate and coat each herring evenly with the oatmeal, pressing it in gently.

Place the fish on a grill rack and grill for 3–4 minutes on each side until the skin is golden brown and the flesh flakes easily. Serve hot with green beans and the mustard sauce.

LOBSTER THERMIDOR

Dijon is the traditional mustard to use in this classic dish as it contrasts beautifully with the lobster.

Serves 2–4

2 live lobsters (about 675g/1 1/2lb each)

25ml/1 1/2 tbsp butter

30ml/2 tbsp plain flour

30ml/2 tbsp brandy

120ml/4fl oz/1/2 cup milk

90ml/6 tbsp double cream

15ml/1 tbsp Dijon mustard

lemon juice

*freshly grated Parmesan cheese, for
    sprinkling*

salt and white pepper

fresh parsley and dill sprigs, to garnish

COOK'S TIP

*There are several ways to kill a
lobster humanely, including the
method used here. Alternatively,
immerse the lobster in distilled
water (previously boiled) for 30
minutes or place a cleaver just
behind the head and hammer
down with one sharp blow.*

Bring a large saucepan of salted water to the boil. Put the lobsters into the pan, head first, and cook for 8–10 minutes. Cut the lobsters in half lengthways, discard the dark sac behind the eyes and pull out the string-like intestine from the tail. Remove the meat from the shells, reserving the coral and liver, then rinse the shells and wipe dry. Cut the flesh into bite-size pieces. Set aside.

Melt the butter in a saucepan and stir in the flour. Cook, stirring, until pale, then gradually add the brandy and milk, whisking vigorously to make a smooth sauce. Whisk in the cream and mustard.

Push the lobster coral and liver through a sieve into the sauce and whisk to blend. Reduce the heat and simmer very gently for about 10 minutes, stirring frequently, until thickened. Season with salt, if necessary, and with pepper and lemon juice.

Preheat the grill and arrange the lobster shells in a shallow flameproof dish. Stir the lobster meat into the sauce and divide evenly among the shells. Sprinkle lightly with Parmesan cheese and grill until golden. Serve garnished with herbs.

FISH STEAKS WITH MUSTARD SAUCE

All sorts of fish can be perked up with a lively mustard sauce. Halibut or turbot is delicious for a special meal, but cod or haddock is also excellent.

Serves 4–6

*4–6 halibut or turbot steaks, about
   2.5cm/1in thick*
40g/1¹/₂oz/3 tbsp butter, melted
salt and ground black pepper
*lemon wedges and parsley sprigs,
   to garnish*

For the mustard sauce
*60ml/4 tbsp Dijon or German
   mustard*
*300ml/¹/₂ pint//1¹/₄ cups double or
   whipping cream*
2.5ml/¹/₂ tsp caster sugar
*15ml/1 tbsp white wine vinegar
   or lemon juice*

Preheat the grill. Season the fish steaks with salt and pepper and arrange them on an oiled rack. Brush the tops of the steaks with melted butter and grill for 4–5 minutes on each side until tender, turning once and brushing with more butter.

Meanwhile, to make the sauce, blend the mustard, cream, sugar and vinegar or lemon juice in a small, heavy-based saucepan and bring to boiling point, stirring constantly. Do not allow to boil, but simmer gently for 1–2 minutes until the sauce thickens, continuing to stir all the time. Remove from the heat and keep warm. Transfer the fish to warmed plates and spoon the sauce over. Serve at once, garnished with lemon wedges and parsley.

BREAM WITH MUSTARD AND BUTTER

Sea bream, with its fabulous creamy flavour, is enhanced by the flavours of Dijon mustard and fennel and served with a rich mustard and butter sauce.

Serves 2

*2 sea bream, about 350g/12oz each,
    scaled and cleaned*

10ml/2 tsp Dijon mustard

5ml/1 tsp fennel seeds

30ml/2 tbsp olive oil

50g/2oz watercress

*175g/6oz mixed salad leaves, such as
    curly endive or oakleaf lettuce*

orange segments, to garnish

jacket potatoes, to serve

For the mustard and butter sauce

*30ml/2 tbsp frozen orange juice
    concentrate*

*175g/6oz/³⁄₄ cup unsalted butter,
    diced*

5–10ml/1–2 tsp Dijon mustard

salt and cayenne pepper

Preheat a moderate grill and slash the fish four times on each side. Blend together the mustard and fennel seeds and spread over both sides of each fish. Brush with a little olive oil and then grill the fish for about 6 minutes on each side until tender.

Put the orange juice concentrate into a heatproof bowl and heat over 2.5cm/1in of boiling water in a pan. Reduce the heat and gradually add the pieces of butter, a few at a time, whisking until they are all incorporated and the sauce is creamy. Whisk in the mustard and seasoning to taste.

Moisten the watercress and salad leaves with the remaining olive oil. Place the fish on two serving plates with the leaves. Garnish with orange segments, pour over the sauce and serve with jacket potatoes.

MUSTARD AND DILL PLAICE

This tangy sauce will give a Scandinavian flavour to all sorts of grilled fish dishes.

Serves 4

4 fillets of plaice, lemon sole or
   Dover sole
40g/1¹/₂oz/3 tbsp butter, melted
salt and ground black pepper
slices of lemon and dill sprigs,
   to garnish

For the sauce

25g/1oz/2 tbsp butter
20g/³/₄oz/1¹/₂ tbsp plain flour
300ml/¹/₂ pint/1¹/₄ cups hot
   fish stock
15ml/1 tbsp white wine vinegar
45ml/3 tbsp chopped fresh dill
15ml/1 tbsp wholegrain mustard
10ml/2 tsp sugar
2 egg yolks, lightly beaten

Skin the fish if preferred and check to make sure there are no hidden bones. If there are, remove them with tweezers.

To make the sauce, melt the butter in a saucepan and stir in the flour. Cook for 1–2 minutes over a low heat, stirring, and then gradually stir in the hot fish stock. Bring to the boil, stirring all the time, and simmer for 2–3 minutes. Reduce the heat and beat in the vinegar, dill, mustard, sugar and seasoning to taste. Slowly beat in the egg yolks. Continue beating over a very low heat for a further minute and then keep warm while cooking the fish.

Preheat the grill to high and place the fish on an oiled grill rack. Brush the fish with a little melted butter and season with salt and pepper. Grill for 4–6 minutes. Carefully turn the fish over, brush again with butter and grill for a further 4–6 minutes until the fish is cooked through and the flesh flakes easily. Arrange the fish on warmed serving plates and pour the sauce over. Garnish with lemon slices and dill and serve.

COOK'S TIP
When grilling fish it is best not to remove the skin, as this helps keep the shape of the fish.

Home-made Mustards

Mustard has long been used by cooks for pickling vegetables, making chutneys and relishes and for creating uniquely flavoured mustards. Enjoyable and satisfying, a home-made mustard is wonderful to serve on special occasions or to give as an unusual but delicious gift.

BREAD-AND-BUTTER MUSTARD PICKLES

This is a traditional American pickle with cucumber and onions pickled in a distinctive blend of whole white mustard seeds and an array of spices.

Makes about 1.75kg/4–4 ½lb

900g/2lb cucumbers, cut into
    5mm/¼ in slices
2 onions, thinly sliced
50g/2oz/¼ cup salt
350ml/12fl oz/1 ½ cups cider
    vinegar
350g/12oz/1 ½ cups sugar
30ml/2 tbsp white mustard seeds
10ml/2 tsp celery seeds
2.5ml/½ tsp ground turmeric
2.5ml/½ tsp black peppercorns

Place the cucumbers and onions in a large bowl, add the salt and mix well. Fit a plate inside the bowl, pressing down on the mixture. Add a weight to compress the vegetables even more and leave for 3 hours. Drain the cucumber and onions, rinse under cold running water and drain again.

Place the vinegar, sugar, mustard seeds, celery seeds, ground turmeric and peppercorns in a large saucepan. Bring to the boil, stirring to dissolve the sugar. Add the drained cucumber and onions, bring to the boil and then immediately remove from the heat. Spoon the pickle into warm sterilized preserving jars, making sure the vegetables are covered with the liquid. Cover with airtight lids and store for at least one month before using.

HONEY MUSTARD

Delicious, aromatic, home-made mustards mature to the most fragrant of relishes. This honey mustard is richly flavoured and is wonderful in sauces and salad dressings.

Makes about 500g/1¼lb

225g/8oz/1 cup mustard seeds
15ml/1 tbsp ground cinnamon
2.5ml/½ tsp ground ginger
300ml/½ pint/1¼ cups white wine vinegar
90ml/6 tbsp dark clear honey

Mix the mustard seeds with the spices and pour on the vinegar. Leave to soak overnight and then place the mixture in a mortar and pound until you have made a paste, adding the honey gradually as you pound the mixture. The finished mustard should resemble a stiff paste. If too stiff, add a little extra vinegar. Store the mustard in four sterilized labelled jars in the fridge and use within four weeks.

HORSERADISH MUSTARD

This is a tangy relish that is an excellent accompaniment to cold meats, smoked fish or cheese.

Makes about 400g/14oz

30ml/2 tbsp mustard seeds
115g/4oz/½ cup dry mustard
115g/4oz/½ cup sugar
120ml/4fl oz/½ cup white wine vinegar or cider vinegar
60ml/4 tbsp olive oil
5ml/1 tsp lemon juice
30ml/2 tbsp horseradish sauce

Place the mustard seeds in a bowl and pour over 250ml/8fl oz/1 cup boiling water. Leave for 1 hour and then drain and place in a blender or food processor with the dry mustard, sugar, vinegar, olive oil, lemon juice and horseradish sauce. Blend the mixture to a smooth paste and spoon into sterilized jars. Label and store in the fridge and use within three months.

CLOVE-SPICED MUSTARD

Making your own mustard is surprisingly easy and, just as with other freshly ground spices, the flavour is more intense and aromatic than that of the shop-bought version.

Makes about 300ml/½ pint/1¼ cups

75g/3oz/6 tbsp white mustard seeds

50g/2oz/¼ cup soft light brown sugar

5ml/1 tsp salt

5ml/1 tsp black peppercorns

5ml/1 tsp cloves

5ml/1 tsp ground turmeric

200ml/7fl oz/⅞ cups distilled malt vinegar

COOK'S TIP

Store for up to 2 weeks before tasting. Store unopened jars for up to 2 months in a cool place.

Place the mustard seeds, sugar, salt, peppercorns, cloves and turmeric in a blender or food processor and process until evenly blended. Gradually add the vinegar, 15ml/1 tbsp at a time, blending well between each addition, then continue blending until you have a coarse paste.

Leave to stand for 10–15 minutes to thicken slightly and then spoon into a sterilized 300ml/½ pint/1¼ cup jar or several smaller jars. Cover the surface of the mustard with a waxed paper disc and then seal with a screw-topped lid or cork and label and date.

MUSTARD AND THYME CRACKERS

These aromatic crisp crackers are perfect served with hard or cream cheese.

Makes about 40

*175g/6oz/1½ cups plain wholewheat
    flour*

50g/2oz/½ cup oatmeal

25g/1oz caster sugar

10ml/2 tsp baking powder

15ml/1 tbsp fresh thyme leaves

50g/2oz/4 tbsp butter

25g/1oz/2 tbsp white vegetable fat

45ml/3 tbsp milk

10ml/2 tsp Dijon mustard

30ml/2 tbsp sesame seeds

salt and ground black pepper

Preheat the oven to 200°C/400°F/Gas 6. Mix together the flour, oatmeal, sugar, baking powder, thyme and seasoning and then rub in the butter and vegetable fat. Blend the milk and mustard together and stir into the flour mixture. Continue stirring to make a soft, but not sticky dough.

Knead the mixture lightly on a floured surface, then roll out to a 5mm/¼in thickness. Cut out 5cm/2in rounds and place, spaced slightly apart, on two greased baking sheets. Prick the rounds with a fork and sprinkle with sesame seeds. Bake for 10–12 minutes until lightly browned. Cool completely before serving. The crackers will keep for up to five days in an airtight jar or tin.

INDEX